Billy at school

Story by Jenny Giles

Illustrations by Betty Greenhatch

Billy said,

"I like walking to school

with you, Jack."

"But you can't stay here with us,"

said a big girl.

"You are not a school boy."

Mom said,

"You will be 5

on your birthday, Billy."

Jack said,

"And you can come to school."

Billy saw Anna on the slide.

"Can I go and play
with Anna?" he said.

"I have to go
and see Jack's teacher,"
said Mom.

"I will look after Billy for you,"
said Anna's mom.

"Oh, thank you," said Mom.
"I will come back
and get you, Billy."

Billy played on the slide with Anna.

Mom went inside with Jack.

All the big boys and girls
went into school.

A teacher said to Billy,
"The bell has rung.
Go into school, please."

"But I'm not a school boy,"
said Billy. "I'm 4."

"Oh!" said the teacher.

"You look like a **school** boy!"

Mom came back to get Billy.

Billy said,

"Mom! The teacher said

I look like a **school** boy!"